ADVANCED VOCABULARY GAMES

for English Language Learners

ADVANCED VOCABULARY GAMES

for English Language Learners

Linda Schinke-Llano

National Textbook Company
a division of NTC/CONTEMPORARY PUBLISHING COMPANY
Lincolnwood, Illinois USA

To The Teacher

The blackline masters in
this book may be
photocopied or
reproduced using infrared
copying techniques.

ISBN: 0-8442-7396-1

Published by National Textbook Company,
a division of NTC/Contemporary Publishing Group, Inc.,
4255 West Touhy Avenue,
Lincolnwood (Chicago), Illinois 60646-1975 U.S.A.
© 1987 by NTC/Contemporary Publishing Group, Inc.

8 9 ML 9 8 7 6

CONTENTS

TO THE TEACHER

The enclosed set of blackline masters contains 32 word games designed for advanced students of English as a second or foreign language at the junior and senior high school levels. Intended as supplementary activities, the games can be used to review and reinforce everyday vocabulary, including verbs and useful expressions. Individual pages may be employed immediately following related lessons in basal series, or later as spot-checks to see if students have retained the information presented in daily lessons. Appropriate for individual as well as group work, the vocabulary games can be utilized in class or as brief take-home assignments. They are especially useful in the mixed-level class which is so prevalent in ESL programs. In all instances, the activities are intended to provide students with an enjoyable alternative for review and to save teachers time by supplying ready-to-use supplementary material.

Basal ESL series commonly used at the junior and senior high school levels were consulted in order to keep vocabulary and structures appropriate for the targeted groups. Whenever possible, items are presented in context in an effort to aid comprehension and retention. At times the context is deliberately cultural, since learning a second language involves learning a second culture as well. All pages have directions, and the majority have examples for the students. Most games are self-correcting; in addition, answers for each game are provided in the Answer Key section of this book.

With respect to directions to the students, an effort was made to keep the language as simple as possible, especially in earlier pages. Certain expressions, however, are unavoidable. Therefore, it is suggested that the teacher include an explanation of key directional terms prior to assigning activities. Since comprehension of directions is crucial to completing assignments correctly, this preparation will help students not only with the vocabulary games in this book, but also with assignments in their content area classes. Words and expressions used frequently in the directions are as follows:

Fill in...   Blanks
Circle...   Underlined words
List...   Parentheses
Unscramble...   Correct form
Match...   Verbs
Answer the questions...
Read...
Draw a line...
Put in order...
Rewrite...

Twelve different types of games are used, as well as combinations and variations of several. If students are unfamiliar with such word games, it may be necessary to work through some of the most common as group activities. The following are suggested:

1. *Anagrams:* (See #15 as an example.) Anagrams are presented in context to assist students in decoding.

2. *Hidden words:* (See #13.) Such puzzles are based on a theme. Words in the puzzle may be found horizontally, vertically, and diagonally, as well as forward and backward.

3. *Fill-ins:* (See #14.) Fill-in items are presented in context. Several activities include the pool of words from which the student will choose.

4. *Fit-ins:* (See #8.) Fit-ins are self-correcting. In addition, most fit-in puzzles spell out a theme word or phrase when correctly finished or are coupled with numerically referenced puzzles.

5. *Inside words:* (See #11.) Words chosen are related to a theme. Students make new words by recombining letters of the cue word. Although many new words could be made from each cue, it is expected that students will find the most common letter combinations. Therefore, they are asked to make a minimal number of words for each cue. This exercise is useful in acquainting students with word formation practices in English, and teachers may wish to expand the activity if students are successful with it.

6. *Crossword puzzles:* (See #1.) Puzzles are related to a theme to aid students in identifying the proper words. The words "across" and "down" are used instead of "horizontal" and "vertical."

For less advanced classes, the author has created two companion books of blackline masters, *Easy Vocabulary Games for Beginning English Language Learners* and *Vocabulary Games for Intermediate English Language Learners.* In addition, students will find it helpful to use the *Everyday American English Dictionary,* also published by National Textbook Company, with all three books of vocabulary games.

ANSWER KEY

Master 1: OCCUPATIONS

Across:
3. nurse
4. jockey
5. janitor
9. principal
11. lawyer
12. tailor

Down:
1. president
2. cook
6. astronaut
7. ballerina
8. miner
10. actor

Master 2: HEADLINES

1. N
2. E
3. W
4. S
5. P
6. A
7. P
8. E
9. R
10. S

NEWSPAPERS

Master 3: CONTINENTS AND COUNTRIES

ASIA
1. Thailand
2. Korea
3. China

AFRICA
1. South Africa
2. Kenya
3. Morocco

EUROPE
1. Poland
2. Spain
3. Austria

NORTH AMERICA
1. Canada
2. Mexico
3. United States

SOUTH AMERICA
1. Brazil
2. Peru
3. Venezuela

Master 4: ENGLISH CLASS

left column, top to bottom:
parentheses
exclamation point
quotation marks
colon
semicolon
brackets
question mark
comma
dash
apostrophe

Master 5: DIRECTIONS

Main and Washington

Master 6: PREPOSITIONS

1. Y
2. O
3. U
4. R
5. E
6. R
7. I
8. G
9. H
10. T

YOU'RE RIGHT!

Master 7: CITY LIFE

Across:
1. subway
4. store
6. concert
8. parade
11. police

Down:
1. skyscraper
2. highway
3. crowd
5. theater
7. traffic
8. park
9. noise
10. zoo

Master 8: ABBREVIATIONS

1. UNITED STATES
2. FEBRUARY
3. JUNIOR
4. REVEREND
5. TELEVISION
6. FRIDAY
7. GALLON
8. FEET
9. MINUTE
10. POUND
11. INCH
12. SOPHOMORE
13. CAPTAIN
14. DOCTOR
15. OUNCE
16. MILE
17. JANUARY
18. THURSDAY
19. OKAY
ABBREVIATIONS ARE EASY!

Master 9: SIGNS

NO VACANCY — motel
S. TAYLOR, D.D.S. — dentist's office
DEER CROSSING — state park
1979 SEDAN — used-car lot
Men's Clothing — department store
HOME 12, VISITORS 7 — football field
VISITING HOURS — hospital
EXPRESS PASSENGERS — train station
SLOW, MEN WORKING — highway
DANGER! THIN ICE — pond
Next Teller Please — bank
Adults $3.00, Children $1.50 — movie theater

K. MARTIN, M.D. — doctor's office
SELF-SERVE — gas station
For Long Distance — telephone booth
Everything Fresh Daily — bakery

Master 10: RELATIONSHIPS

1. A *pedestrian* isn't involved with the law.
2. A *reverend* isn't a military person.
3. *Neighbors* aren't relatives.
4. A *cashier* isn't an educator.
5. An *actor* isn't a musician.
6. A *citizen* isn't a public official.
7. An *officer* isn't a religious person.
8. A *passenger* isn't a driver.
9. A *teller* doesn't work in a restaurant.
10. An *usher* isn't involved in sports.
11. An *audience* doesn't perform.
12. An *architect* doesn't work the land.

Master 11: SCIENCE CLASS

Astronomy:	*Chemistry:*
my	chest
roast	mist
storm	try
roomy	them
star	trim

Test Tube:	*Experiment:*
best	mix
but	rim
stub	men
tub	prime
beet	time

Bacteria:	*Beaker:*
race	bake
cab	rake
rib	beer
cart	bare
tab	ear

X

Master 12: WORDS FOR MALES AND FEMALES

1. MRS
2. ACTRESS
3. GIRL
4. HEIRESS
5. WOMAN
6. NUN
7. DAUGHTER
8. FEMALE
9. QUEEN
10. MOTHER
11. AUNT
12. LANDLADY
13. NIECE
14. WIFE
15. HOSTESS
16. PRINCESS
17. LADY
18. SISTER

Master 13: COUNTRY LIFE

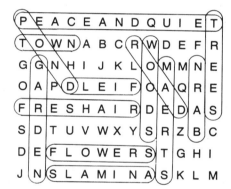

peace and quiet
pond
town
field
stream
garden
barn
woods
flowers
animals
road
fresh air
trees

Master 14: IRREGULAR PAST TENSE

was, heard, tried
hit, fell, broke, took
froze, fed, did, bit
hid, caught, put
flew, thought
spent, had, set, stole
got, tore
became, could
ran

Master 15: WEIGHTS AND MEASURES

height
weight
length, width
depth
distance
temperature

1. ounces
2. ton
3. pint
4. gallon
5. mile
6. centimeters
7. kilogram
8. pounds
9. inch
10. degrees

Master 16: CROSSWORD SYNONYMS

Across:
1. have
3. timid
5. finish
6. present
7. pail
8. yes
11. follow
12. fat
14. huge
16. false
17. run
18. us
19. start

Down:
1. happy
2. afraid
3. tiny
4. intelligent
9. store
10. bother
12. folks
13. cash
15. fast

Master 17: FORMS AND FIGURES

left column, top to bottom:
wavy line
octagon
stripes
dotted line
checks
cube
perpendicular lines

right column, top to bottom:
plaid
cylinder
diagonal line
polka dots
zigzag
pentagon
parallel lines

Master 18: AT THE LIBRARY

1. LIBRARY
2. LIBRARIAN
3. CATALOG
4. SHELF
5. CHECK OUT
6. RENEW
7. FICTION
8. BIOGRAPHY
9. DICTIONARY
10. ENCYCLOPEDIA
YOUR BOOK IS OVERDUE!

Master 19: AT THE BEACH
1. bathing suit, sandals
2. beach towel, lawn chair
3. crab, lobster, clams
4. sailboat, yacht, rowboat
5. seashells
6. swimming, sunbathing
7. seaside, seashore

Master 20: ANTONYMS

1.	F	7.	C
2.	I	8.	E
3.	A	9.	G
4.	B	10.	D
5.	K	11.	J
6.	L	12.	H

Master 21: LANGUAGES OF THE WORLD

Across:
1. Vietnamese
5. Japanese
6. Russian
7. Greek
8. English
11. Swedish
12. Dutch
13. Chinese
14. Korean
15. French

Down:
2. Turkish
3. Spanish
4. Portuguese
9. Italian
10. German

Master 22: IRREGULAR PAST PARTICIPLES

1.	taught	7.	risen
2.	begun	8.	lain
3.	grown	9.	drawn
4.	cost	10.	sworn
5.	ridden	11.	beaten
6.	held	12.	built

PAST PARTICIPLES ARE HARD.

Master 23: MIXED-UP SENTENCES

1. My brother just bought a "new" car.
2. Unfortunately it's a 1968.
3. It has 115,000 miles on it.
4. It's very rusty.
5. The passenger door and the trunk don't open.
6. The windshield wipers don't work.
7. The horn works, but it's very quiet.
8. The radio is missing.
9. And the engine makes noise.
10. Do you know anyone who wants to buy a car?

Master 24:   ANOTHER WORD FOR . . .

1. auto
2. sack
3. pocketbook
4. infant
5. couch
6. trousers
7. carpet
8. chair
9. baggage
10. motion picture
11. corridor
12. pastime
13. billfold
14. stream
15. attorney

Master 25:   MATH CLASS

algebra		minus
arithmetic		multiply
decimal		number
denominator		numerator
divide		percent
equation		plus
geometry		subtract
mathematics		

Master 26:   IN THE MOUNTAINS

1. peak
2. hike
3. camp
4. sleeping bag
5. tent
6. cabin
7. trail
8. forest
9. backpack
10. axe
11. campfire
12. lantern
13. canoe
14. waterfall
15. wildlife

Master 27:   ELECTRONIC AGE

Satellite:	*Computer:*
sat	put
tell	come
let	mop
tea	cut
tile	rope

Video Game:	*Calculator:*
dive	call
move	act
gave	roll
dime	all
mad	out

Master 28:   WORDS AND THEIR FUNCTIONS

Thanking:
1. I really appreciate this.
2. I'm very grateful.

Accepting Thanks:
1. It was my pleasure.
2. Don't mention it.
3. I was glad to do it.

Complaining:
1. This food is terrible!
2. Why are you always late?

Introducing:
1. This is John.
2. Have you met Ken?
3. I'd like you to meet Lois.

Promising:
1. I won't let you down.
2. I swear I'll do it.

Complimenting:
1. You did a great job.
2. I really like your dress.
3. What a good dancer!

Deciding:
1. Give me a minute.
2. Let me think about that.

Apologizing:
1. I'm really sorry.
2. Can you forgive me?
3. I didn't mean to do it.

Master 29:   LEISURE TIME

collect
*coins, *stamps, *postcards
*matchbooks, *butterflies
*jogging
*tennis, *bicycling, *skiing,
   *swimming
sports
paint, draw
build, sew
activities
Note: The order of these items may
be changed within the paragraph.

Master 30:   TWO-WORD VERBS

1. over
2. off
3. in
4. on
5. over
6. over
7. out
8. up
9. back
10. up
11. by
12. down
13. in
14. off
15. in

Master 31:   TREASURE HUNT

1. Have you ever been on a treasure hunt?
2. Eight of us went on one last Saturday.
3. We met at Anthony's house.
4. First we were sent to the playground.
5. We found a clue under the basketball hoop.
6. That clue sent us to the ice-cream shop.
7. There we found a clue in our ice cream.
8. Then we were sent to the movie theater.
9. Finally we were sent back to Anthony's.
10. At his house we found the treasure—a party for all of us.

Master 32:   FORMAL AND INFORMAL WORDS

1. K
2. D
3. G
4. A
5. N
6. H
7. B
8. O
9. C
10. I
11. M
12. L
13. E
14. F
15. J

NTC ESL/EFL TEXTS AND MATERIAL

Computer Software
Basic Vocabulary Builder on Computer

Language-Skills Texts
*English with a Smile 1, 2
*The English Survival Series
  Building Vocabulary A, B, C
  Identifying Main Ideas A, B, C
  Recognizing Details, A, B, C
  Writing Sentences and Paragraphs
  A, B, C
*English across the Curriculum 1, 2, 3
*Everyday English 1, 2, 3, 4
*Everyday Consumer English
Play and Practice!
Reading by Doing
Writing by Doing
Speaking by Doing
Building Real Life English Skills
Everyday American English Dictionary
Building Dictionary Skills in English
 (workbook)

High-Interest Readers
*Passport to America Series
  California Discovery
  Adventures in the Southwest
  The Coast-to-Coast Mystery
  The New York Connection

Language and Culture Readers
Discover America Series (text/audio-cassette)
  New York
  Chicago
  California
  Florida
  Washington D.C.
  New England
  Hawaii
  Texas
*Looking at American Signs
*Looking at American Food
*Looking at American Recreation
*Looking at American Holidays

Text/Audiocassette Learning Packages
*Speak Up! Sing Out! 1, 2
*Listen & Say It Right in English!

Duplicating Masters
Easy Vocabulary Games
Vocabulary Games
Advanced Vocabulary Games
Play and Practice!
Basic Vocabulary Builder
Practical Vocabulary Builder

*Published by Voluntad Publishers, Inc.,
a subsidiary of National Textbook
Company

For further information or a current catalog, write:
National Textbook Company
4255 West Touhy Avenue
Lincolnwood, Illinois 60646-1975 U.S.A.

1. OCCUPATIONS

DIRECTIONS: Fill in the crossword puzzle with the names of occupations.

Across

3. someone who helps the doctor take care of people who are ill

4. a person who rides a horse in a race

5. a person who cleans a building and carries keys to the doors

9. the person in charge of a school

11. a person who takes care of another person's legal matters

12. someone who makes or changes the fit of suits, coats, or pants

Down

1. the head of a government or other organization

2. a person who cooks food

6. someone who travels in space

7. a female ballet dancer

8. someone who works in a mine

10. a man or boy who acts in a play or film

2. HEADLINES

DIRECTIONS: Circle the letter of the section of the newspaper where you can find the headline. Then write the letters in the blanks at the bottom of the page.

Example: **SOX WIN 3–0!**

A. weather

B. sports

C. front page

1. **U.S. AND RUSSIA TO TALK**

   M. financial section

   N. world news

   O. local news

2. *Stock Up 3 Points*

   E. financial section

   F. editorial

   G. sports

3. **A BUY AT $72,500**

   V. employment

   W. real estate

   X. world news

4. **Cold Front Expected**

   Q. entertainment

   R. local news

   S. weather

5. **MAYOR WINS REELECTION**

   N. world news

   O. TV section

   P. local news

6. **Fall Programming Starts Tonight**

   A. TV section

   B. sports

   C. weather

7. **A New Bestseller**

   N. local news

   O. financial section

   P. book section

8. **Olympic Runners Set Records**

   D. front page

   E. sports

   F. entertainment

9. *COMPUTERS A PROMISING FIELD*

   R. employment

   S. world news

   T. local news

10. **Singer Makes Debut**

    R. world news

    S. entertainment

    T. local news

___ ___ ___ ___ ___ ___ ___ ___ ___ ___
1　2　3　4　5　6　7　8　9　10

3. CONTINENTS AND COUNTRIES

DIRECTIONS: Unscramble the names of the continents. Then list the countries under their correct continent.

Example: **LATAARSIU** _____ Australia _____

SAAI _____

1. _____
2. _____
3. _____

AIRCAF _____

1. _____
2. _____
3. _____

REPUOE _____

1. _____
2. _____
3. _____

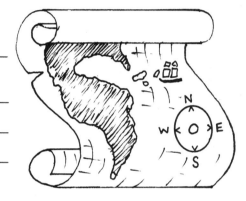

TONRH RAMICEA _____

1. _____
2. _____
3. _____

SHOUT RICEAMA _____

1. _____
2. _____
3. _____

Canada	Spain
Poland	Kenya
Thailand	Morocco
Brazil	Venezuela
Korea	United States
South Africa	Austria
Mexico	China
Peru	

4. ENGLISH CLASS

DIRECTIONS: Draw a line from the punctuation mark on the left to its name on the right.

Example: •——————— period

( )   quotation marks

!   brackets

" "   dash

:   colon

;   exclamation point

[ ]   parentheses

?   comma

,   apostrophe

——   semicolon

→'s   question mark

5. DIRECTIONS

DIRECTIONS: Read the paragraph. Then answer the question. Use the map to help you.

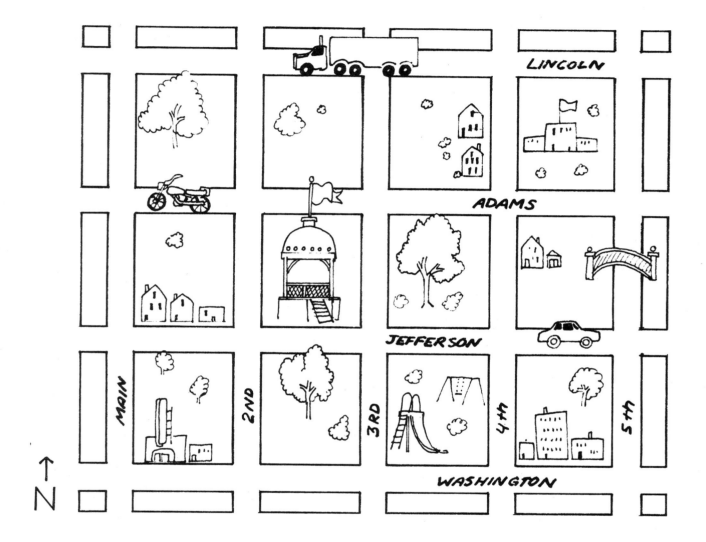

You are at the corner of Main and Washington. Walk north two blocks. Turn right. Walk three blocks. Turn left for one block. Turn left again and walk for one block. Turn south and walk for two blocks. Turn right and walk two more blocks. Then go south for one block. What corner are you at?

_____

6. PREPOSITIONS

DIRECTIONS: Circle the letter of the correct choice. Then write the letters in the blanks at the bottom of the page.

Example: He put his hand _____ the glove.

    A. from

    (B.) in

    C. to

1. I got a letter _____ him.

    X. at

    Y. from

    Z. around

2. The dog stayed _____ his house.

    O. inside

    P. through

    Q. from

3. _____ John, this is right.

    S. Behind

    T. Toward

    U. According to

4. Carol walked _____ the crowd.

    P. on

    Q. under

    R. through

5. Walk _____ that house.

    E. toward

    F. on

    G. according to

6. Is your sister _____ home?

    R. at

    S. in

    T. to

7. Do you live _____ school?

    H. below

    I. near

    J. on top of

8. Mike sat _____ Ruth.

    F. to

    G. next to

    H. at

9. Leave your boots _____ the door.

    F. in

    G. on

    H. outside

10. Please give this _____ him.

    S. from

    T. to

    U. at

__ __ __ ’ __ __ __ __ __ __ __ !
1 2 3 4 5 6 7 8 9 10

7. CITY LIFE

DIRECTIONS: Fill in the crossword puzzle with words relating to life in the city.

Across

1. an underground electric train

4. a place where things are sold

6. a performance of musical compositions

8. a lot of people walking or marching together

11. people who enforce the law

Down

1. a very tall building

2. a public road where cars move at high speed

3. a lot of people together in one place

5. a building where plays are performed

7. cars, buses, and trucks moving along the street

8. an open place with grass and trees

9. a very loud or unpleasant sound

10. a place where wild animals are kept for people to look at

8. ABBREVIATIONS

DIRECTIONS: The word on the left is an abbreviation. Write the complete word on the right. Then write the circled letters in the blanks at the bottom.

Example: Mr.   M I S T E R

1. U.S.   _ _ _ _ _ _   _ _ Ⓞ _ _
2. Feb.   _ _ Ⓞ _ _ _ _
3. Jr.   _ _ _ _ _ Ⓞ _
4. Rev.   _ Ⓞ _ _ _ _ _
5. TV   _ _ _ _ Ⓞ _ _ _
6. Fri.   _ _ Ⓞ _ _ _
7. gal.   _ Ⓞ _ _ _ _
8. ft.   _ _ _ Ⓞ _
9. min.   _ Ⓞ _ _ _ _
10. lb.   _ Ⓞ _ _ _
11. in.   _ Ⓞ _ _
12. Soph.   Ⓞ _ _ _ _ _ _ _ _
13. Capt.   _ _ _ _ Ⓞ _ _
14. Dr.   _ _ _ _ _ Ⓞ
15. oz.   _ _ _ Ⓞ _
16. mi.   _ _ Ⓞ _ _
17. Jan.   _ _ _ _ Ⓞ _ _
18. Thurs.   _ _ _ Ⓞ _ _ _
19. OK   _ _ Ⓞ

_B_ _ _ _ _ _ _ _ _ _ _ _   _ _ _   _ _ _ _ !
1   2 3 4 5 6 7 8 9 10 11 12   13 14 15   16 17 18 19

9. SIGNS

DIRECTIONS: Draw a line between the sign and the place where you find it.

Example:

| QUIET PLEASE | ———————— library |

NO VACANCY

S. TAYLOR, D.D.S.

DEER CROSSING

**1979 SEDAN
ONLY $1,099!**

Men's Clothing
4th Floor

| HOME | VISITORS |
| 12 | 7 |

VISITING HOURS
4–8 pm

EXPRESS
PASSENGERS
STAND HERE

dentist's office

highway

gas station

football field

motel

pond

state park

used-car lot

bank

doctor's office

bakery

department store

train station

movie theater

hospital

telephone booth

SLOW
MEN WORKING

DANGER!
THIN ICE

Next Teller Please

Adults $3.00
Children $1.50

K. MARTIN, M.D.

SELF-SERVE

For Long Distance
Dial 0 + Number

Everything
Fresh Daily

10. RELATIONSHIPS

DIRECTIONS:　　Circle the word that doesn't belong. Then tell why it doesn't.

Example:　　doctor　dentist　(clerk)　nurse

　　　　　　　A clerk isn't a medical person.

1.　judge　lawyer　juror　pedestrian　_____

2.　Captain　Reverend　Lieutenant　Major　_____

3.　parents　daughter　neighbors　in-laws　_____

4.　professor　teacher　tutor　cashier　_____

5.　violinist　actor　drummer　pianist　_____

6.　citizen　president　king　prime minister　_____

7.　monk　priest　nun　officer　_____

8.　chauffeur　engineer　passenger　bus driver　_____

9.　teller　waiter　cashier　hostess　_____

10.　usher　coach　player　referee　_____

11.　singer　audience　dancer　actor　_____

12.　landscaper　gardener　architect　farmer　_____

11. SCIENCE CLASS

DIRECTIONS: Make new words from the words below.

Example: **ATOM**

_____ at _____

_____ mat _____

ASTRONOMY

TEST TUBE

BACTERIA

_____

_____

_____

_____

_____

_____

_____

_____

CHEMISTRY

EXPERIMENT

BEAKER

12. WORDS FOR MALES AND FEMALES

DIRECTIONS: A word used for males is on the left. Fill in the blanks with a similar word used for females.

Example: masculine   F E M I N I N E

1. Mr.

2. actor

3. boy

4. heir

5. man

6. priest

7. son

8. male

9. king

10. father

11. uncle

12. landlord

13. nephew

14. husband

15. host

16. prince

17. gentleman

18. brother

13. COUNTRY LIFE

DIRECTIONS: There are thirteen words or phrases in the puzzle relating to life in the country. Circle them. Then write them on the lines at the bottom of the page.

Example: O F (M R A F) O N _____farm_____

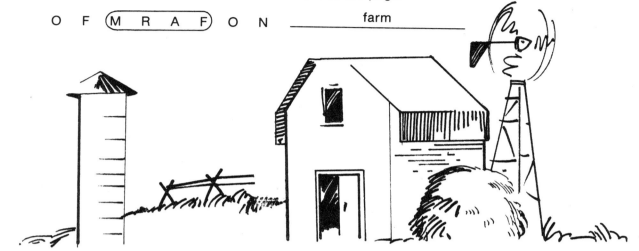

```
P E A C E A N D Q U I E T
T O W N A B C R W D E F R
G G N H I J K L O M M N E
O A P D L E I F O A Q R E
F R E S H A I R D E D A S
S D T U V W X Y S R Z B C
D E F L O W E R S T G H I
J N S L A M I N A S K L M
```

_____   _____

_____   _____

_____   _____

_____   _____

_____   _____

_____

Name _____ Date _____

14. IRREGULAR PAST TENSE

DIRECTIONS: Fill in the blanks with the past tense of the verbs in parentheses.

Example: He __ran__ a mile in six minutes.
            (run)

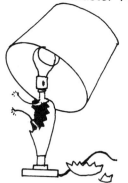

Yesterday _____ a bad day! I _____ the alarm at 7:00 a.m. When I _____ to turn it off,
          (be)   (hear)   (try)

I _____ the lamp and it _____ off the table and _____. Then I _____ a shower, but there was
  (hit)   (fall)   (break)   (take)

no hot water. I _____! Next I _____ the dog, but he _____n't like his food, so he _____
               (freeze)   (feed)   (do)   (bite)

my tennis shoe and _____ in the bushes. I finally _____ him and _____ him in the house.
                   (hide)   (catch)   (put)

Then I _____ to catch the 7:48 bus for school. I _____ I had exact change, but I didn't.
       (fly)   (think)

So I _____ more than I _____ to. I _____ my books on the seat, and someone _____ them.
     (spend)   (have)   (set)   (steal)

When I _____ off the bus, I _____ my jacket on the door.
       (get)   (tear)

When I looked at the school yard, I didn't see anyone. I _____ worried. I _____n't be that late!
                                                         (become)   (can)

I _____ to the door and bumped into the janitor. "What are you doing here on a Saturday?" he asked.
  (run)

Some days it doesn't pay to get up!

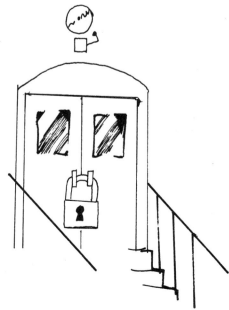

15. WEIGHTS AND MEASURES

DIRECTIONS: Unscramble the letters to make a word.

Example: <u>Measures</u>
            (ASERMUSE)

We use weights and measures daily. For example, if we

want to know how tall someone is, we want to know

the person's _____. When we ask how much a
            (TEGHIH)

person weighs, we are talking about _____.
                                      (WETHIG)

If we want to know the size of a swimming pool, we

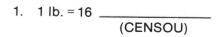

measure the _____, _____,
              (NETGLH)   (HIDTW)

and _____.
      (PETHD)

If we ask how far it is from one city to another, we are

talking about _____. And finally, when we discuss
               (TENSADCI)

the weather, we talk about the _____.
                                 (PETMETREARU)

1. 1 lb. = 16 _____   6. 1 meter = 100 _____
                (CENSOU)   (METRESTNICE)

2. 2,000 lbs. = 1 _____   7. 1,000 grams = 1 _____
                    (NOT)   (RAGMILOK)

3. 2 cups = 1 _____   8. 1 kilogram = 2.2 _____
                (NITP)   (SUNPOD)

4. 4 quarts = 1 _____   9. 2.54 centimeters = 1 _____
                  (NAGLOL)   (CHIN)

5. 5,280 ft. = 1 _____   10. freezing = 0 _____ Celsius
                   (LIME)   (SEDGERE)

16. CROSSWORD SYNONYMS

DIRECTIONS: Fill in the crossword puzzle with synonyms of the words given.

Example: simple E A S Y

	Across		*Down*
1. own	12. heavy; overweight	1. content; not sad	
3. bashful, shy	14. enormous	2. scared	
5. end	16. fake; not true	3. very small	
6. gift	17. jog	4. smart	
7. bucket	18. him and me	9. a shop	
8. affirmative	19. begin	10. annoy	
11. pursue		12. people	
		13. money	
		15. quick	

17. FORMS AND FIGURES

DIRECTIONS: Draw a line from the figure to its name.

Example:  ——————— circle

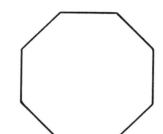

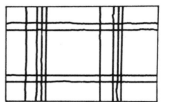

plaid

octagon

wavy line

checks

cylinder

diagonal line

stripes

dotted line

perpendicular lines

polka dots

zigzag

pentagon

cube

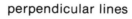

parallel lines

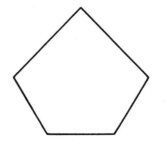

18. AT THE LIBRARY

DIRECTIONS: Unscramble the letters to make a word. The definition will help you. Then fill in the numbered blanks at the bottom of the page with the correct letters.

Example: something you read   <u>B O O K</u> (OKOB)

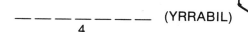

1. a room or building full of books

— — — — <u>—</u> — — (YRRABIL)
       4

2. a person who is trained to work in a library

— — — — — — — — (AAIIRRLBN)
    5   13

3. a list of books in a library

— — — — — — — (TAGLOAC)
       11

4. a place where books are put

— — — — — (FLESH)
10 15

5. to borrow a book from a library

— — — — — — — (ECCKH TUO)
      8   3

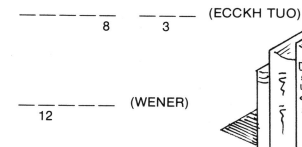

6. to get permission from a librarian to borrow a book for a time longer than you had asked for at first

— — — — — (WENER)
12

7. a made-up story or book about people and happenings that are not really true

— — — — — — (ONITCIF)
       2

8. the story of a person's life written by another person

— — — — — — — — — (PARGHYIOB)
    7   1

9. a book that tells you the meanings of words and how to spell them

— — — — — — — — — — (NARTICDIOY)
     9

10. a book or set of books that tells something about every subject

— — — — — — — — — — — — (CLOPIADEENCY)
      6   14

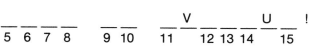
— — — —   — — — —   — — ^V—   — ^U— — !
1 2 3 4   5 6 7 8   9 10   11   12 13 14   15

19. AT THE BEACH

DIRECTIONS: Answer the questions. Use the words at the bottom of the page to help you.

Example: Name a place where there is a lot of sand. ____beach____

1. Name two items of clothing you wear at the beach.

    a. _____ b. _____

2. Name two things you sit on at the beach.

    a. _____ b. _____

3. Name three kinds of seafood.

    a. _____ b. _____ c. _____

4. Name three water vehicles.

    a. _____ b. _____ c. _____

5. Name something that people collect at the beach.

    a. _____

6. Name two activities that people do at the beach.

    a. _____ b. _____

7. Give two other names for the beach.

    a. _____ b. _____

seaside	lobster	yacht	seashore
bathing suit	beach	sandals	swimming
beach towel	sunbathing	lawn chair	seashells
clams	sailboat	crab	rowboat

20. ANTONYMS

DIRECTIONS: Read the sentences. Then match the words at the bottom of the page with their antonyms.

Example: Jason left the party early.

___Z___ early   Z. late

1. Susan wore a very fancy dress.
2. Please combine these papers.
3. Ted is a very sincere person.
4. The dancer was very clumsy.
5. What a wonderful movie!
6. The fruit is very sour.
7. Will this material shrink?
8. The car was stationary.
9. The old tree was very twisted.
10. The characters in the story were imaginary.
11. What a gloomy picture!
12. Did you thaw the bacon?

_____ 1. fancy	A. dishonest
_____ 2. combine	B. graceful
_____ 3. sincere	C. stretch
_____ 4. clumsy	D. real
_____ 5. wonderful	E. moving
_____ 6. sour	F. plain
_____ 7. shrink	G. straight
_____ 8. stationary	H. freeze
_____ 9. twisted	I. separate
_____ 10. imaginary	J. cheerful
_____ 11. gloomy	K. terrible
_____ 12. thaw	L. sweet

21. LANGUAGES OF THE WORLD

DIRECTIONS: Fill in the crossword puzzles with the names of languages.

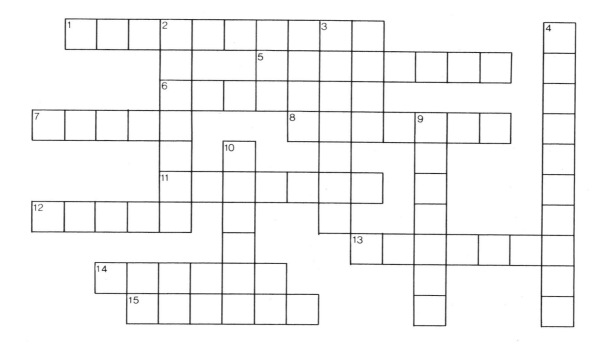

Across

A language spoken in:

1. Vietnam   11. Sweden

5. Japan   12. the Netherlands

6. Russia   13. China

7. Greece   14. Korea

8. Canada   15. France

Down

A language spoken in:

2. Turkey

3. Mexico and
     Puerto Rico

4. Brazil

9. Italy

10. Germany

22. IRREGULAR PAST PARTICIPLES

DIRECTIONS: Fill in the blanks with the past participle of the verb in parentheses. Then write the correct letters in the numbered blanks.

Example: I have __known__ him for many years.
(know)

K N O W N
‾ ‾ ‾ ‾ ‾

1. Mr. Simon has _____ English for 10 years.
(teach)

‾ ‾ ‾ ‾ ‾ ‾
13   3

2. Class had _____ on time.
(begin)

‾ ‾ ‾ ‾ ‾
11

3. The baby has _____ four inches since birth.
(grow)

‾ ‾ ‾ ‾ ‾
14

4. That building has _____ too much already.
(cost)

‾ ‾ ‾ ‾
8

5. Have you _____ a horse before?
(ride)

‾ ‾ ‾ ‾ ‾
7 19 15

6. Melissa is being _____ by her father.
(hold)

‾ ‾ ‾ ‾
16 10

7. My grandfather has _____ every morning at 6 a.m. for
(rise)
40 years.

‾ ‾ ‾ ‾ ‾
5   12

8. Has the dog _____ there long?
(lie)

‾ ‾ ‾ ‾
1

9. The Statue of Liberty has been _____ many times.
(draw)

‾ ‾ ‾ ‾
18 4

10. The man had _____ to tell the truth.
(swear)

‾ ‾ ‾ ‾ ‾
2

11. Have the Bears _____ the Jets before?
(beat)

‾ ‾ ‾ ‾ ‾
17

12. George had _____ the house before he got married.
(build)

‾ ‾ ‾ ‾ ‾
9   6

P ‾ ‾ ‾   P ‾ ‾ ‾ ‾ ‾ ‾   P ‾ ‾ ‾   ‾ ‾ ‾   ‾ ‾ ‾ ‾
  1 2 3   4 5 6 7 8 9   10 11 12   13 14 15   16 17 18 19

23. MIXED-UP SENTENCES

DIRECTIONS: Unscramble the sentences. Rewrite them on the lines at the bottom of the page. Be sure to punctuate the new sentences correctly.

Example: a car / have / Do you _Do you have a car?_

1. a "new" car / bought / just / My brother
2. a 1968 / Unfortunately / it's
3. 115,000 miles / It has / on it
4. rusty / very / It's
5. don't open / and the trunk / The passenger door
6. work / The windshield wipers / don't
7. it's / The horn / but / very quiet / works
8. is / missing / The radio
9. makes / And / noise / the engine
10. a car / Do you know / who wants / anyone / to buy

1. _____

2. _____

3. _____

4. _____

5. _____

6. _____

7. _____

8. _____

9. _____

10. _____

24. ANOTHER WORD FOR . . .

DIRECTIONS: Unscramble the letters to make a word.

Example: Another word for valise is ____suitcase____ .   (SEATCUSI)

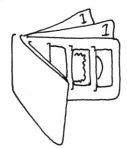

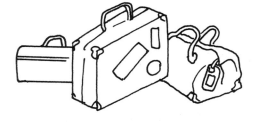

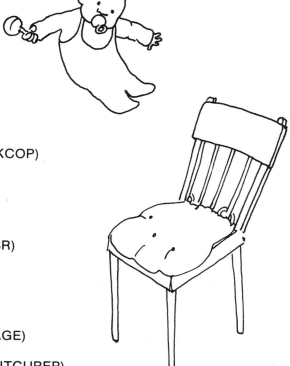

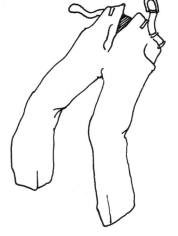

1. Another word for car is _____ .   (TOUA)

2. Another word for bag is _____ .   (KASC)

3. Another word for purse is _____ .   (BETKOOKCOP)

4. Another word for baby is _____ .   (TANFIN)

5. Another word for sofa is _____ .   (OCCHU)

6. Another word for pants is _____ .   (SETORUSR)

7. Another word for rug is _____ .   (TEARPC)

8. Another word for seat is _____ .   (ARCHI)

9. Another word for luggage is _____ .   (GAGBAGE)

10. Another word for movie is _____ .   (OTIMNO ITCUREP)

11. Another word for hallway is _____ .   (DOORRIRC)

12. Another word for hobby is _____ .   (SEATMIP)

13. Another word for wallet is _____ .   (FILLBLOD)

14. Another word for creek is _____ .   (RESTAM)

15. Another word for lawyer is _____ .   (TOREYANT)

25. MATH CLASS

DIRECTIONS: There are fifteen math words hidden in the puzzle. Circle them. Then write them on the lines at the bottom of the page.

Example: X O (A D D) F   _____ add _____

```
M U L T I P L Y A B D E C
A R I T H M E T I C E Q N
T D D I V I D E N E C U U
H F G H I N J K U L I A M
E M N O P U Q R M S M T E
M P T U V S W X B Y A I R
A L G E B R A Z E Z L O A
T U A B C F P E R C E N T
I S D G G E O M E T R Y O
C M D E N O M I N A T O R
S U B T R A C T P E F G H
```

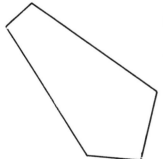

a+b=c

_____   _____   _____

_____   _____   _____

_____   _____   _____

_____   _____   _____

_____   _____   _____

26. IN THE MOUNTAINS

DIRECTIONS: Use the words at the bottom of the page to complete the sentences.

Example: A very high hill is called a ___mountain___ .

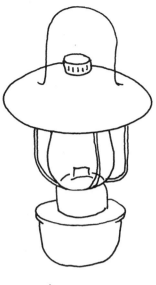

1. The top of a mountain is its _____ .
2. To walk through the mountains is to _____ .
3. To sleep outdoors is to _____ .
4. A _____ is like a bed.
5. A shelter made of canvas is a _____ .
6. A _____ is a small house made of logs.
7. A path through the woods is a _____ .
8. Another word for woods is _____ .
9. To carry things on your back, you use a _____ .
10. To cut down trees, you use an _____ .
11. You cook your meal over a _____ .
12. You use a _____ to see at night.
13. A light, narrow boat that is pointed at both ends is a _____ .
14. A stream of water flowing from a high place is a _____ .
15. Animals in the forest are called _____ .

trail	mountain	waterfall	camp
canoe	campfire	forest	wildlife
hike	sleeping bag	peak	cabin
backpack	axe	tent	lantern

27. ELECTRONIC AGE

DIRECTIONS: Make new words from the words below.

Example: **STEREO**

_____ see _____

_____ rest _____

SATELLITE

_____ _____
_____ _____
_____ _____
_____ _____
_____ _____
_____ _____

VIDEO GAME

_____ _____
_____ _____
_____ _____
_____ _____
_____ _____
_____ _____

COMPUTER

_____ _____
_____ _____
_____ _____
_____ _____
_____ _____

CALCULATOR

_____ _____
_____ _____
_____ _____
_____ _____
_____ _____

28. WORDS AND THEIR FUNCTIONS

DIRECTIONS: List the expressions under the functions they serve.

Example: **THANKING**

Thank you very much.

This is John.
I'm really sorry.
I won't let you down.
I swear I'll do it.
You did a great job.
I really like your dress.
What a good dancer!

Give me a minute.
Have you met Ken?
Can you forgive me?
I didn't mean to do it.
I'd like you to meet Lois.
I really appreciate this.
It was my pleasure.

This food is terrible!
Why are you always late?
Don't mention it.
Let me think about that.
I'm very grateful.
I was glad to do it.

THANKING

1. _____
2. _____

PROMISING

1. _____
2. _____

ACCEPTING THANKS

1. _____
2. _____
3. _____

COMPLIMENTING

1. _____
2. _____
3. _____

COMPLAINING

1. _____
2. _____

DECIDING

1. _____
2. _____

INTRODUCING

1. _____
2. _____
3. _____

APOLOGIZING

1. _____
2. _____
3. _____

29. LEISURE TIME

DIRECTIONS: Fill in the blanks with words from the bottom of the page. (Note: Be sure the paragraphs make sense.)

Example: See the first sentence.

People do different things with their ____leisure____ time. Many people _____ things.

For example, some collect _____ or _____. Others collect _____

or _____. And some collect _____.

Many people use their leisure time for sports. For example, _____ is very popular.

So are _____ and _____. Others prefer _____ and _____.

Some people don't like collecting or _____. They may use their leisure time for

arts and crafts. For example, some people like to _____ or _____ pictures.

Others _____ furniture or _____.

What are your favorite _____ for leisure time?

paint	sports	draw
tennis	jogging	stamps
collect	leisure	bicycling
matchbooks	butterflies	coins
skiing	swimming	postcards
build	sew	activities

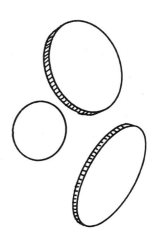

30. TWO-WORD VERBS

DIRECTIONS: Fill in the blanks with a word from the bottom of the page. (Note: Words may be used more than once.)

Example: Sit <u>d o w n</u>, please.

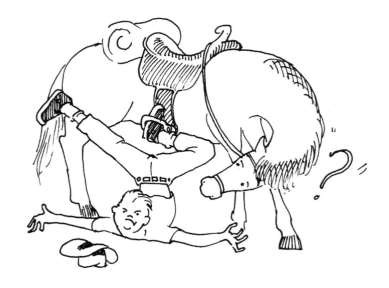

1. She turned the rock __ __ __ slowly.

2. The plane took __ __ __ on time.

3. Tune __ __ station KXYZ.

4. Keep __ __ talking.

5. Let's go __ __ __ __ these answers.

6. Don't trip __ __ __ __ the toys.

7. Would you pass __ __ __ these papers?

8. Look __ __ the word in the dictionary.

9. Please give __ __ __ __ the book.

10. Call him __ __ again.

11. Let's stop __ __ Jean's house.

12. Copy __ __ __ __ these numbers.

13. Hand __ __ your papers tomorrow.

14. He got __ __ __ the horse on the wrong side.

15. Fill __ __ the blanks.

off	on	over
up	down	in
back	by	out

31. TREASURE HUNT

DIRECTIONS: Put the sentences in order to make a story. Then write the story in the blanks at the bottom of the page.

We found a clue under the basketball hoop.

Then we were sent to the movie theater.

We met at Anthony's house.

That clue sent us to the ice-cream shop.

Eight of us went on one last Saturday.

First we were sent to the playground.

Have you ever been on a treasure hunt?

There we found a clue in our ice cream.

At his house we found the treasure—a party for all of us.

Finally we were sent back to Anthony's.

1. _____

2. _____

3. _____

4. _____

5. _____

6. _____

7. _____

8. _____

9. _____

10. _____

32. FORMAL AND INFORMAL WORDS

DIRECTIONS: Match the underlined formal word on the left with an informal word on the right. Write the letter in the blank.

Example: __Z__   He's a nice child.   Z.   kid

_____ 1. "How old are you?" he inquired.   A. breathing

_____ 2. "Fourteen," she stated.   B. ready

_____ 3. They terminated their friendship.   C. bought

_____ 4. His respiration is normal.   D. said

_____ 5. I wish you good fortune.   E. house

_____ 6. The nurse gave me an injection.   F. started

_____ 7. Are you prepared?   G. ended

_____ 8. The couple quarreled.   H. shot

_____ 9. My father purchased a new car.   I. dishes

_____ 10. Grandma used her best china.   J. drink

_____ 11. Your stockings don't match.   K. asked

_____ 12. What an intelligent dog!   L. smart

_____ 13. Is that your residence?   M. socks

_____ 14. Who initiated this conversation?   N. luck

_____ 15. Whose beverage is this?   O. argued